KWANZAA

by A. P. Porter
pictures by Janice Lee Porter

Carolrhoda Books, Inc. / Minneapolis

To colored people everywhere — A.P.P.

These pictures are dedicated with love and gratitude to Jai, Amenah, Sindiswa, Damani, Namibia, and Charise, and to all children whose roots still feed them from Africa — J.L.P.

And thanks to Gwenyth Swain, our editor, and Ken Nelson, the designer — A.P.P. and J.L.P.

This book is available in two editions:
Library binding by Carolrhoda Books, Inc.
Soft cover by First Avenue Editions
241 First Avenue North
Minneapolis, Minnesota 55401

Library of Congress Cataloging-in-Publication Data

Porter, A. P.
    Kwanzaa / by A.P. Porter ; pictures by Janice Lee Porter.
      p.   cm. — (Carolrhoda on my own book)
    Summary: Describes the origins and practices of Kwanzaa, an African-American holiday created to remind African Americans of their history and their cultural origins.
    ISBN 0-87614-668-X (lib. bdg.)
    ISBN 0-87614-545-4 (pbk.)
    1. Kwanzaa — Juvenile literature. 2. Afro-Americans — Social life and customs — Juvenile literature. [1. Kwanzaa. 2. Afro-Americans — Social life and customs.] I. Porter, Janice Lee, ill. II. Title. III. Series.
GT4403.A2P67 1991
394.2'68 — dc20   90-28605
                                                                  CIP
                                                                  AC
Manufactured in the United States of America

            4   5   6   7   8   9   10   00   99   98   97   96   95   94   93

Table of Contents

New Words

Author's note: Kwanzaa is an African-American holiday. Many of the words used at Kwanzaa time come from Swahili—also called Kiswahili—an African language. Each Swahili word is printed in **bold** type the first time it comes up in this story.

bendera (behn-DEH-rah): a flag for African Americans

Habari gani? (hah-BAH-ree GAH-nee): What's new?

Harambee! (hah-rahm-BEH): Let's pull together!

imani (ee-MAH-nee): believing in yourself

karamu (kah-RAH-moo): the feast

kikombe cha umoja (kee-KOM-beh chah oo-MOH-jah): the cup of togetherness

kinara (kee-NAH-rah): the candle holder

kujichagulia (koo-ji-chah-goo-LEE-ah): acting and speaking for yourself

kuumba (koo-OOM-bah): thinking of new ways to do things

Kwanzaa (KWAHN-zah): an African-American holiday. From the phrase "ya kwanza," which means "first."

Kwanzaa yenu iwe na heri! (KWAHN-zah YEH-noo EE-weh nah HEH-ree): May your Kwanzaa be happy!

mazao (mah-ZAH-oh): the fruits and vegetables

mishumaa saba (mee-shoo-MAH SAH-bah): the seven candles

mkeka (mm-KEH-kah): the place mat

muhindi (moo-HIN-dee): the corn

nguzo saba (nn-GOO-zoh SAH-bah): the seven reasons, or principles, behind Kwanzaa

nia (NEE-ah): having a reason, or purpose, for doing what you do

Swahili (swah-HEE-lee), also called Kiswahili (ki-swah-HEE-lee): a language of East Africa

ujamaa (oo-jah-MAH): going to each other to buy services and to buy things

ujima (oo-JEE-mah): working together

umoja (oo-MOH-jah): staying together, or unity

zawadi (zah-WAH-dee): the gifts

Kwanzaa is an
African-American holiday.
Kwanzaa honors black people
and their history.

7

An African-American teacher
named Maulana Karenga
created Kwanzaa in 1966.
Dr. Karenga wanted to teach
his people about their history.

He wanted to teach them
about African ways and holidays.
He created Kwanzaa
to remind his people
of their African beginnings.

African-American history
is older than the United States.
In the 1600s,
white people forced Africans
to go to North America as slaves.
Those African slaves are
the ancestors
of most black Americans.

Slaves are people
who are owned by other people.
Slave owners can do anything
they want to their slaves.
They can beat them.
They can make them work.
They can kill them.

For two hundred years,
most African Americans were slaves.
Slaves in America became free in 1863.
The law said freed slaves could do
whatever they wanted,
but black Americans did not have
the same rights as other Americans.

African Americans could live
only near other black people.
They could go to school
only with other black people.
They could go to church
only with other black people.
They could be buried
only with other black people.

In the early 1900s,
a leader of black people
named Marcus Garvey
created a flag—the **bendera**.
The black bar in the center stands
for black people staying together.
Red is for their long struggle
for fairness and freedom.
Green stands for the future.
When Dr. Karenga created Kwanzaa,
he remembered the bendera
and what it meant.

At Kwanzaa time,
African Americans think
about their people,
their struggles,
and their future.

HARRIET TUBMAN

Kwanzaa lasts for seven days,
from December 26 to January 1.
African Americans start to get ready
for Kwanzaa early in December.
They gather together
the seven symbols of Kwanzaa.
A symbol is something that stands
for something else.

The first symbol is the **mkeka**,
or place mat.
The mkeka may be an African mat.
It can even be made by hand,
from strips of cloth or paper.
The mkeka is a symbol of history.
Today stands on yesterday,
the way the other symbols stand
on the mkeka.

A big cup,
the **kikombe cha umoja**,
is a symbol of staying together.
Everyone sips juice or wine
from the kikombe
at Kwanzaa time.

People also put **mazao**,
or fruits and vegetables,
on the mkeka.
Mazao stand for the harvest
and for all work.
When African Americans put
fruits and vegetables on the mkeka,
they honor themselves
and their work.

The **muhindi**, or corn,
stands for children.
A family puts one ear of corn
on the mkeka for each child.
But even if there are no children,
people have muhindi on their mkeka.

The **kinara**, or candle holder,
is the heart of a Kwanzaa setting.
The kinara stands for people
who lived many years ago in Africa.
Africans hold up African Americans,
just as the kinara holds candles.

The kinara's seven candles
are called the **mishumaa saba**.
Candles light the way.
A black candle is in the center.
Three red candles are on the left,
and three green candles on the right.

The **zawadi**, or gifts,
are the last Kwanzaa symbols.
Zawadi are for the children.
Zawadi are rewards
for promises kept during the year.

When all of the symbols are ready,
it's time to decorate.
Kwanzaa decorations are mostly
black, red, and green,
the colors of the bendera
and the mishumaa saba.
Sometimes people put a bendera
on the wall nearby.
They put the mkeka on a low table.
Then they arrange the kikombe, mazao,
muhindi, kinara, and mishumaa saba
on the mkeka.
The zawadi are placed off
to the side until later.

Kwanzaa is especially for children.
On the first day of Kwanzaa,
a child lights the black candle
in the center of the kinara.
One more candle is lit each day,
starting with the red candle
and then the green candle
closest to the center.
When the day's candles are lit,
the child talks about one
of the reasons for Kwanzaa.

In Swahili,

these reasons are called

the **nguzo saba**—the seven principles.

A principle is a reason for being.

The nguzo saba are goals

for African Americans to strive for.

On each day of Kwanzaa,

children talk about

one of the seven principles.

Many people put a copy

of the nguzo saba on the wall

at Kwanzaa time.

The nguzo saba are written out

at the end of this book.

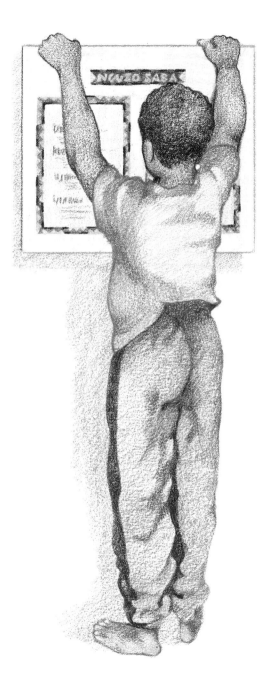

During Kwanzaa,
people greet each other in Swahili.
They say, "**Habari gani?**"—
"What's the news?"
The answer is the principle
for that day.
So, on the first day,
the answer to "Habari gani?"
is "**Umoja!**"
Umoja means unity.
Unity is staying together.
A child lights the black candle
in the center of the kinara.
Starting with the oldest people,
everybody sips from the kikombe.
Then the child who lit the candle
talks about what umoja means.

31

Slave owners seldom let
slave families stay together.
Slaves could be sold
or sent away at any time.
Many children did not know
their parents or sisters or brothers.
They did not feel a part of anything
except slavery.

Many African Americans are still not
part of a community.
People who work, live,
and build a future together
create a community.
A strong community is the reward
for people who practice umoja.

"Habari gani?" someone asks.
On the second day of Kwanzaa,
the answer is "**Kujichagulia!**"
For African Americans,
kujichagulia is saying who they are
and who they will be.
A child lights the black candle
and a red candle—for struggle.
Then the child talks of kujichagulia.

35

As slaves,
African Americans had no power.
They could not name themselves.
Their owners named them.
They could not make decisions.
Their owners decided for them.

African Americans must act
and speak for themselves,
no matter what others may say.
With kujichagulia,
African Americans are
no one's slaves.

37

On the third day,
friends say, "Habari gani?"
Everyone responds, "**Ujima!**"
The chosen child lights
the black candle, the red candle,
and a green candle—for the future.
Then the child talks of ujima,
which means helping each other
by working together.

To African Americans,
selfishness is wrong.
To do better as a group,
African Americans should work
on their problems together.
Ujima makes even a heavy load
easy to carry.

Someone asks, "Habari gani?"
On the fourth day of Kwanzaa,
people say, "**Ujamaa!**" in reply.
A child lights the first three
candles and another red one.
Ujamaa means buying
from each other.
African Americans buy most things
from people who are not black.
Going to stores and clinics
owned by black people
makes the African-American
community stronger.
Ujamaa is sharing the wealth
of all black people.

41

"Habari gani?"
The answer for the fifth day
of Kwanzaa is "**Nia!**"
A child lights the first four candles
and another green candle.
Nia means purpose.
The purpose of African Americans
is to make their people great.
Africa is very old.
The world's first communities
were African.
But slavery made African Americans
forget their past.
At Kwanzaa time,
black Americans remember
their past and their purpose—
to make their people great.

"Habari gani?"
On the sixth day of Kwanzaa,
"**Kuumba!**" is the answer.
A child lights the first five
candles, then the last red one.
Kuumba means creativity.
Creativity is thinking
of new ways to do things.
Alice Walker uses kuumba
to write books.

In Africa, people use kuumba
to make their communities strong.
To make their world better,
African Americans use
their creativity, too.

45

The **karamu**, or feast,
is held on December 31,
the sixth day of Kwanzaa.
The food is arranged
on a big mkeka
in the middle of the floor.

People help themselves.
Everyone tries to bring
some food to share,
no matter how little.
Some people have no food to bring,
but no one cares.
Everyone is welcome.

"Habari gani?"

"**Imani!**" is the answer
on the last day of Kwanzaa.
All of the candles are lit in order,
ending with the last green candle.
Imani means faith.
Imani is believing in
all African people.

Some people hate African Americans.
They think that black Americans
do not deserve the same rights
as other Americans.
But no matter what others may think,
black people must have imani,
faith in themselves.

49

On the last day of Kwanzaa,

each worthy child is given zawadi.

After opening the gifts,

everyone says "**Harambee!**" seven times.

Harambee means to pull together.

Near the end of the last day,

everyone drinks again from the kikombe.

They remember Africans

and African Americans

who helped black people.

Sometimes they make a speech:

May we live by the nguzo saba.

May the year's end meet us

laughing and stronger.

And at the end of next year,

may more of us sit together.

May we achieve a better life.

Kwanzaa teaches everyone
about Africa and African culture.
Kwanzaa is also about the history
and future of African Americans.
Kwanzaa can help all people
understand African Americans.
And it can help black children
understand themselves.

At Kwanzaa time,
black people and their friends
get together and remember.
Kwanzaa yenu iwe na heri!
May your Kwanzaa be happy!

NGUZO SABA

Umoja (Unity)
To strive for and maintain unity in the family, community, nation, and race.
Umoja means staying together.

Kujichagulia (Self-Determination)
To define ourselves, name ourselves, create for ourselves, and speak for ourselves, instead of being defined, named, created for, and spoken for by others.
Kujichagulia is saying who we are and who we will be, and not letting others say for us.

Ujima (Collective Work and Responsibility)
To build and maintain our community together, and make our sisters' and brothers' problems our problems; and to solve our problems together.
Ujima means working together and helping each other.

Ujamaa (Cooperative Economics)
To build and maintain our own stores, shops, and other businesses, and to profit from them together.
Ujamaa means buying from each other.

Nia (Purpose)
To make our collective vocation the building and developing of our community, in order to restore our people to their traditional greatness.
Nia means making our people as great as they can be.

Kuumba (Creativity)
To do always as much as we can, in the way we can, in order to leave our community more beautiful and beneficial than we inherited it.
Kuumba means thinking of ways to make our community better.

Imani (Faith)
To believe with all our hearts in our people, our parents, our teachers, our leaders, and the righteousness and victory of our struggle.
Imani means believing in ourselves and the worth of our people.

by Maulana Karenga
with additions by A. P. Porter

What You Need to Celebrate Kwanzaa

The gifts and symbols of Kwanzaa don't need to cost a lot of money. The ideas matter, not the things.

Kwanzaa is a young holiday and is celebrated differently in different parts of the country. Start with this basic list of ingredients, and your Kwanzaa celebration can become richer every year. Begin gathering things early in December, so you will be ready for the first day of Kwanzaa, on December 26.

1. a place mat—the mkeka: You can buy an African mat or make one yourself from woven paper or cloth.
2. a cup—the kikombe cha umoja: Any large cup will do.
3. fruits and vegetables—the mazao: Use apples, potatoes, oranges—all the fruits and vegetables you like best.
4. a candle holder—the kinara: Be sure there are spaces for seven candles.
5. seven candles—the mishumaa saba: Any candles will do, but you will need one black candle, three red ones, and three green candles.
6. corn—muhindi: Gather as many ears of corn as there are children at your Kwanzaa celebration.
7. gifts—zawadi: Simple gifts are good. Zawadi need not be from a store. Books and handmade things are good Kwanzaa gifts.
8. the flag for African Americans—the bendera: If you don't have a bendera, be sure to decorate for Kwanzaa in the bendera's colors—red, black, and green.
9. a copy of the seven reasons for Kwanzaa—the nguzo saba: You will find the nguzo saba on pages 54 and 55 of this book. Use the nguzo saba in your Kwanzaa setting.